Kenneth E. Hagin

## Chapter 1
## THE GLORY IN THE OLD TESTAMENT

*But he* [Stephen, the first martyr], *being full of the Holy Ghost, looked up stedfastly into heaven, and saw THE GLORY OF GOD, and Jesus standing on the right hand of God.*
— Acts 7:55

We frequently *feel* the glory of God in manifestation among us. And as we walk with God, we're conscious of His glory, and we're changed from glory to glory. But in Acts 7:55, it says Stephen *saw* something. What did he see?

The Jews who heard Stephen preach this sermon in Acts 7 well understood what Stephen meant when he said he saw the glory of God. There are many references to the glory of God in the Old Testament, beginning with these from Exodus.

## EXODUS 16:7,10
7 And in the morning, then ye shall see THE GLORY OF THE LORD; for that he heareth your murmurings against the Lord....
10 And it came to pass, as Aaron spake unto the whole congregation of the children of Israel, that they looked toward the wilderness, and, behold, THE GLORY OF THE LORD appeared in the cloud.

## EXODUS 40:34,35
34 Then a cloud covered the tent of the congregation, and THE GLORY OF THE LORD filled the tabernacle.
35 And Moses was not able to enter into the tent of the congregation, because the cloud abode thereon, and THE GLORY OF THE LORD filled the tabernacle.

## LEVITICUS 9:4,6,23
4 Also a bullock and a ram for peace offerings, to sacrifice before the Lord; and a meat offering mingled

with oil: for to day the Lord will appear unto you. . . .
6    And Moses said, This is the thing which the Lord
commanded that ye should do: and THE GLORY OF
THE LORD shall appear unto you. . . .
23 And Moses and Aaron went into the tabernacle
of the congregation, and came out, and blessed the
people: and THE GLORY OF THE LORD appeared
unto all the people.

NUMBERS 14:10
10 But all the congregation bade stone them with
stones. And THE GLORY OF THE LORD appeared
in the tabernacle of the congregation before all the
children of Israel.

NUMBERS 20:6
6    And Moses and Aaron went from the presence of
the assembly unto the door of the tabernacle of the
congregation, and they fell upon their faces: and THE
GLORY OF THE LORD appeared unto them.

1 KINGS 8:10,11
10 And it came to pass, when the priests were come
out of the holy place, that the cloud filled the house
of the Lord,
11 So that the priests could not stand to minister
because of the cloud: for THE GLORY OF THE
LORD had filled the house of the Lord.

2 CHRONICLES 5:11-14
11 And it came to pass, when the priests were come
out of the holy place: (for all the priests that were

present were sanctified, and did not then wait by course:

12 Also the Levites which were the singers, all of them of Asaph, of Heman, of Jeduthun, with their sons and their brethren, being arrayed in white linen, having cymbals and psalteries and harps, stood at the east end of the altar, and with them an hundred and twenty priests sounding with trumpets:)

13 It came even to pass, as the trumpeters and singers were as one, to make one sound to be heard in praising and thanking the Lord; and when they lifted up their voice with the trumpets and cymbals and instruments of musick, and praised the Lord, saying, For he is good; for his mercy endureth for ever: that then the house was filled with a cloud, even the house of the Lord;

14 So that the priests could not stand to minister by reason of the cloud: for THE GLORY OF THE LORD had filled the house of God.

2 CHRONICLES 7:1,2

1 Now when Solomon had made an end of praying, the fire came down from heaven, and consumed the burnt offering and the sacrifices; and THE GLORY OF THE LORD filled the house.

2 And the priests could not enter into the house of the Lord, because THE GLORY OF THE LORD had filled the Lord's house.

That glory is what Stephen saw, and the Jews he was preaching to understood what he meant. They knew that the glory of the Lord had appeared and filled the House of God. They knew that it often looked like a cloud filling the House, so they understood what Stephen was talking about when he said he saw the glory of the Lord.

Whether you ever see the glory of God in manifestation in this life, when you leave this earth, that's where you're going: to the glory world. Psalm 73:24 says, *"Thou shalt guide me with thy counsel, and afterward receive me to GLORY."*

There is a glory world, and sometimes that glory world is manifested in this world. When it is, it is by a supernatural manifestation of the power of God.

## Chapter 2
## I SAW THE GLORY

I know exactly what Stephen saw, because I saw that glory too. You know my testimony: I was born again on the twenty-second day of April, 1933, at 20 minutes until 8 o'clock, on a Saturday night, in the south bedroom of 405 North College Street, in the city of McKinney, Texas. I was bedfast then. Four months later, on August 16, 1933, the temperature reached 106 degrees in the afternoon, and that was in the shade.

We didn't have air conditioning in those days, so the windows and doors of our house were all open to get a little breeze if there was any. But my body was so cold that my family borrowed hot water bottles from the neighbors and placed them around my body, trying to warm me up! They also placed heated bricks wrapped in newspaper and blankets around me.

I knew all morning that I was dying. At 1:30 in the afternoon, my little brother, who was 9 years old, was standing by my bed as death fastened its final throes upon my body. I said to him, "Run and get Momma — quick! I want to tell her goodbye. I'm dying." He ran out of the room like a shot, and that whole room suddenly was filled with a cloud that was brighter than the sun shining on snow. The whole room was filled with that glory.

I left my body, and I ascended. You see, if you're a Christian when you leave here, you go up. If you're a sinner when you leave here, you go down. The spirit of man is eternal! And there is a spirit world!

I began to ascend in that cloud of glory, and when I got up to about where the roof of the house should be — it was a story-and-a-half building — I heard a voice speak to me in the English language. I believe it was Jesus' voice, although I didn't see Him. But I heard the voice, a man's voice, and it said, "Go back. Go back to the earth. You can't come yet. Your work on earth is not done!"

I descended back down into the room. When I got back, the glory — the cloud — had lifted, and I saw my body for a brief second lying on the bed. I saw my mother standing there holding my hand in hers. I seemed to leap inside my body, like a man would put his foot inside his boot. When I got back inside my body, I could contact Momma, so I said, "Momma, I'm not going to die now!"

She thought I meant I wasn't going to die *at that moment*, but I meant, "I'm not going to die now. I'm going to live and do the work of God." (It was about a year later that I was healed as I acted upon God's Word in faith.)

That experience was so sacred to me that I never shared it with anyone until the Lord instructed me to do so twenty-five years later, in the '50s. The Lord said to me, "Begin to share that experience, and particularly in teaching on 'What It Means To Believe With the Heart.' Establish the fact that the spirit [of man] is eternal, and never dies." So then I began to relate that experience.

In the process of time, we were visiting my mother in my hometown of McKinney, Texas. She was in her late seventies then, and had been blind since I was a small boy. She said, "Son, I heard you teaching on the radio, and I heard you relate that experience. I didn't know about it."

I replied, "Momma, I never told it for many, many years — a quarter of a century — because it was too sacred. Then the Lord said, 'Tell it.'"

(There are one or two more outstanding experiences I have had in the spirit world that I have not been able to share, and I don't know whether God will let me tell about them or not in this life. We can make a great mistake when we talk about things we should be quiet about.

We must be sensitive in our spirit to know and understand whether or not to share them.)

My mother told me, "The way you tell that experience, you were gone maybe a few seconds." I said, "Well, that's what it seemed to me — just a few seconds."

"Well," she said, "let me tell it to you from my standpoint and from Granny's (Granny was her mother). Pat came running back to the kitchen, saying, 'Momma! Momma! Granny! Granny! Ken's dying!' I was nearer to the door, so I rushed up the hallway. When I got to your bedroom door, I couldn't enter the room. I sensed the presence of God, so I backed up by the dining room table and bowed my head and prayed. Your Granny came running after me, and she didn't look inside (the door was open). She tried to run through that glory, and she bounced off it like you would bounce off a rubber ball. She could not enter in."

(Notice in our Scripture reading, the Bible says the priests could not enter in when the glory filled the House of God.)

Momma continued, "Granny backed up about halfway across the dining room and made another run at the open door — and bounced off it like you'd bounce off a giant rubber ball. Then she backed up all the way across the dining room, against the wall on the other side, and made the third run at it — and bounced off again. She couldn't get into that room! She was almost overcome and about to fall because of the glory [notice in the Scriptures, the priests fell when they were in the glory], so she clung to the door frame."

Momma recalled that Granny had said, "Why, Lillie, the room is filled with a cloud! I can't see Ken. I can't see the bed."

And Momma said, "It was ten minutes before we could get into the room. We could not enter the room until all of the cloud had lifted. I continued to stand there by the dining room table, holding onto it and praying, and Granny stood by the door, holding onto the door frame.

"Then Granny said, 'It's beginning to lift. I can see the chair. I can see the chest of drawers. I can see the bed. I can see Ken lying there. His body is lying there on the bed.' But we could not enter into the room until the cloud had completely lifted. Granny couldn't enter at first because she was so overcome — so weak. But she said, 'Well, Lillie, it's all gone. You can enter in now.' "

Momma said, "I rushed to the bed. I picked up your hand and held it. And about that time, you said, 'Momma, I'm not going to die now.' "

That experience was a manifestation of the glory of God, and it was sacred to me. When I thought about it, I realized that there is no such thing as time in the spirit realm. That's why I thought the experience lasted only a few seconds.

From that day to this, I've never felt sorry for Christians who die, whether they're young, middle aged, or old. Yes, I know that healing belongs to us, but we're all going home sometime. I've never felt sorry for them, because I know where they went.

But, oh, it's another story for those who don't know the Lord!

# Chapter 3
## MANIFESTATIONS OF THE GLORY

My second experience with the glory occurred early in my ministry when I was a Baptist boy preacher. I didn't have the baptism of the Holy Spirit yet. One Sunday night I was preaching in a little country church, and my text was from James: *"For what is your life? It is even a vapour, that appeareth for a little time, and then vanisheth away"* (James 4:14).

I had been preaching about fifteen minutes, minding my own business, and suddenly from the back of that little church, I saw this cloud come rolling in. Although it was a cloud, it looked like waves of the ocean about three or four feet high. But it was a cloud! It didn't excite me, because I knew what it was. I had seen it before, on August 16, 1933, the day my spirit had left my body and the cloud filled my bedroom.

When the cloud came into the church, it covered up the people. I couldn't see them. It came as far as the little altar bench and covered it too. And it kept coming. So I looked at my watch and noted the time. The cloud came onto the platform and covered it, and then I couldn't see anything, but I kept preaching. I could hear the sound of my voice, but I couldn't distinguish a word I said. To this day, I don't know a single word I said. That cloud filled the whole church!

Finally it began to lift. It lifted from around the pulpit and the platform first. Then I could see the altar, the front pew, and then the other pews. I was preaching all this time. I could hear the sound of my voice, but I wasn't aware of what I was saying until the cloud left the building. When it lifted, I looked at my watch. The cloud had filled the building for 17 minutes.

I didn't know what to say, because I didn't know what I had been saying! I had been caught up in the glory! So I simply said, "Everyone bow your head, and let's pray." I prayed, gave an invitation, and closed the service as I normally would do. I didn't say anything to anyone that night about having seen the glory cloud.

Two years later, in 1938, I accepted the pastorate of a little Full Gospel church in the blacklands of northcentral Texas. I was single in those days, and I stayed first in the home of one of the deacons. He tried his best to get me interested in a certain young lady there in the church.

One Saturday night, this young lady was

scheduled to sing a special song in our regular Saturday night service, but she didn't show up. Sunday morning as I was preaching, suddenly that glory cloud came in and enveloped me! I couldn't see a person. I couldn't see anything in the congregation. Again, I could hear the sound of my voice, but I couldn't distinguish a single word I said.

I was in that glory, and suddenly I was gone! Right in the middle of my sermon, I found myself standing along a street in a little town fifteen miles away — and I knew it was Saturday night. I was leaning against a building, and I saw this young lady come walking down the street. About the time she got to where I was standing, a car came down the street. The driver pulled up to the curb, sounded the horn, and she got into his car. He backed out, turned the other direction, and started out of town — and suddenly I was sitting in the back seat!

They went out in the country and I saw them commit adultery. I was still in the cloud. Suddenly I heard the sound of my voice, and then the cloud lifted. I was standing behind my pulpit. I didn't know what to say, because I didn't know what I had been saying, so I just said, "Everyone bow your head," and we prayed. I looked at my watch, and again I'd been gone about fifteen minutes in the cloud.

While I was shaking hands with people as they went out the door, this young lady came by. I said, "We missed you last night." She said, "Yes, I was over in ——" (and she named the little town). I said, "Yes, I know."

This was my third experience with the glory. God showed me what she had done just for my own benefit. I dropped her like a hot iron.

The fourth time I experienced a manifestation of God's glory was while I was pastoring that same church. I was walking home after a Wednesday night service.

I was taking a shortcut through an alley that was grown over with trees. It was as dark as could be, but I knew the path through it. As I was walking along, I noticed a car that had been backed into those shadows. A young man and a young lady were in the front seat, and a young man and a young lady were in the back seat of this car. As I walked by, the inside of that car suddenly lit up as if a powerful light bulb had been turned on. The people in the car never saw me or the supernatural light.

One of the young ladies was from my church. I think she was interested in me. I wasn't interested in her, but someone else had tried to get me interested in her. She was sit-

ting on a fellow's lap. He had his arm around
her and that's not all they were doing, but
that's as much as I'll describe. I never told
anyone about that.

You've got to realize, friends, that there is
a fine line between fanaticism and reality. Many
people get off into error seeking experiences.
But these experiences come as the Spirit wills
— not as you will.

The Word of God says in Acts 10:9,10 that
Peter went up on a housetop to pray, and he
fell into a trance. Peter didn't put *himself* into
a trance, and he didn't *try* to go into a trance.

In other religions — in false religions and
cults, for example — people endeavor to go into
a trance. But over in the realm of the Holy
Spirit, when the Spirit of God moves, it is as
*He* wills. You must not try to cause a vision,
trance, or other spiritual experience to happen.
Just let the Holy Spirit do it when and if He
pleases. Just learn to flow with Him.

You should know your Bible well enough to
remember the Old Testament story of Elisha
and Naaman, commander-in-chief of the armies
of Syria (2 Kings 5). Naaman went to Israel
because he wanted to be healed of his leprosy.
The prophet of God didn't even go out of his
house to meet Naaman; he just sent his servant

outside to Naaman, saying, "Go tell him to dip in the River Jordan seven times, and his flesh will become clean again." Naaman finally was persuaded to do so, and he was healed.

In gratitude, Naaman returned to the place where Elisha lived, wanting to give him gifts. Elisha refused his gifts, so Naaman went his way.

But Gehazi, Elisha's servant, ran after Naaman's chariot and overtook him. He lied to Naaman, saying, "You know, after you left, two young prophets came, and although my master would not take anything for himself, he said it would be all right to accept two garments and a talent of silver for each of them."

Naaman was so thrilled to be healed from an incurable condition that he gave Gehazi twice as much as he asked for. Gehazi took the gifts and hid them. Then he went into the presence of Elisha. Elisha said, "Where have you been?" And Gehazi replied, "Nowhere, my master."

Notice Elisha's reply: ". . . *Went not mine heart* [spirit] *with thee, when the man turned again from his chariot to meet thee?*" (v. 26). In other words, Elisha said, "I saw you. I know exactly what you did." Absolutely! So we do have Scripture for these experiences.

## Chapter 4
## HIS GLORY FILLS THE TEMPLE

In Old Testament times, "the House of God" was the physical building. At first it was the *Tabernacle,* which was just a tent. Later, the House of God was called *Solomon's Temple.* It was given that name because Solomon built it. And that's where the Jews met God. (Every male Jew from the age of 30 and older had to present himself at least once a year in the Temple in Jerusalem.)

The presence of God — they called it the *Shekinah* glory — was kept hidden in the Holy of Holies. The glory of the Lord would be manifested in front of the whole congregation, and they would see it.

According to Flavius Josephus, the Jewish historian, the curtain that screened off the Holy of Holies was forty feet wide, twenty feet high, and four inches thick.

But when Jesus died on Calvary, all this changed. Twenty feet in the air, someone took hold of that curtain and ripped it in two from top to bottom! God moved out of the man-made Holy of Holies in the Temple! Now He indwells us individually. *We are each individual temples of the Holy Spirit!* I want to emphasize that, but I also want you to see something else as well:

**HEBREWS 3:6**
6  But Christ as a son over his own house; whose house are we [we collectively make up that house], if we hold fast the confidence and the rejoicing of the hope firm unto the end.

**1 TIMOTHY 3:15**
15  But if I tarry long, that thou mayest know how thou oughtest to behave thyself in the house of God, which is the church of the living God [the house of God is people], the pillar and ground of the truth.

**1 CORINTHIANS 3:16**
16  Know ye not that ye are the temple of God, and that the Spirit of God dwelleth in you?

In other words, Paul is saying, "Know ye not that ye are the House of God?" The people he was addressing — the Corinthians — knew about temples. Their city was filled with all kinds of temples, dedicated to different gods. But Paul is saying, "*You* are the temple of God, and the Spirit of God dwells in you!" John also wrote, "*. . . greater is he that is in YOU, than he that is in the world*" (1 John 4:4).

And it's true! You individually are the temple of God. I like the translation of First

Corinthians 3:16 in *The Amplified Bible*. It begins, "Do you not discern and understand. . . ." Unfortunately, we do *not* discern or understand this fact. ("Discern" also means "to see.")

You could see something without understanding it. I look at television, but I don't understand anything about electronics. So I see it, but I don't understand it.

I remember when we first moved to Tulsa from Garland, Texas. We had bought Brother T. L. Osborn's old office building, and we lived in an apartment above the offices. Our daughter and son-in-law were our only office force. They lived in another apartment above the offices.

I was preaching on radio station KSKY in Dallas at that time. One day I went to the grocery store to get something, and my granddaughter Cookie asked to go with me. I remember we pulled into the parking lot of that grocery store, and I tuned the car radio to KSKY. I noticed Cookie kept looking first at the radio and then at me.

"That's you," she said. "But you're here! That's you. But you're here!"

That was my voice coming out of the radio, but I was sitting there behind the steering wheel! She heard or saw it, but she couldn't understand it.

So we can see or discern many things, but that doesn't necessarily mean we understand them. However, we do need to *understand* as well as *discern*. Let's look at First Corinthians 3:16 again from *The Amplified Bible:* "Do you not discern and understand that you [the whole Church at Corinth] are God's temple (His sanctuary), and that God's Spirit has His permanent dwelling in you — to be at home in you [collectively as a church and also individually]?"

Notice the phrase "His sanctuary." That *body of believers* at Corinth was God's temple or God's house — His sanctuary. The church auditorium that we call the sanctuary may be a "sanctuary" from the standpoint that the building was dedicated to God, but it's not God's sanctuary in the sense that Paul is referring to.

The whole Church at Corinth was God's temple, God's sanctuary, and ". . . God's Spirit has His permanent dwelling in you — to be at home *in you* [collectively as a church and also individually]."

Preachers usually emphasize the fact that the Spirit of God indwells the *individual* Christian — and rightly so. Thank God, greater is He that is in you, than he that is in the world.

Although we do see certain truths about the Spirit indwelling *the whole body of believers,* we still don't understand these truths fully.

We need to discern and understand this: You, *the whole Church* — wherever you are located — are God's temple; His sanctuary. And God's Spirit has His permanent dwelling *in you,* as *The Amplified Bible* brings out, "to be at home in you [COLLECTIVELY AS A CHURCH and also individually]."

We know that the Old Testament shows us "types and shadows," and that Solomon's Temple is a type of this spiritual house, the body of believers. We also saw that the glory of God — the Holy Spirit — came in and filled Solomon's Temple, which was a type of the Body of Christ.

We talk about *individuals* being filled with the Holy Spirit, and rightly so. But, blessed be God, *THAT WHOLE BODY, the Body of Christ, can be filled with the glory of God!*

In studying about this, I noticed that Paul, in Romans 6:4, talking about the resurrection, said: "... *Christ was raised up from the dead by THE GLORY of the FATHER....*" So that same glory which was manifested in the Old Testament raised Christ from the dead!

Another translation says that Jesus was

raised up ". . . by a manifestation of the glory of God." That's what those manifestations were in the Temple throughout the Old Testament: manifestations of the glory of God. *A manifestation of the glory of God is a manifestation of the Spirit of God.*

And in Romans 8:11, Paul writes: *"But if the Spirit of him that raised up Jesus from the dead dwell in you, he that raised up Christ from the dead shall also quicken your mortal bodies by his Spirit that dwelleth in you."*

So we talk about what the Holy Spirit will do in you — what He can mean to you — individually, and that's important. But *we hear and know very little about what the Holy Spirit will do IN THE BODY OF BELIEVERS as a whole because of His indwelling presence.*

The Holy Spirit dwells in you *collectively* — and He wants to come into manifestation! We know that the Holy Spirit manifests Himself in different ways through the gifts of the Spirit, as outlined in First Corinthians 12. But could the Holy Spirit manifest Himself in other ways in the "spiritual house" which Peter says we are: *"Ye also, as lively stones, are built up a spiritual house, an holy priesthood, to offer up spiritual sacrifices, acceptable to God by Jesus Christ"* (1 Peter 2:5)?

Solomon's Temple — that physical building — was built with dead stones. We believers, on the other hand, are called "lively stones." In Old Testament times, there was a priesthood, but Peter says believers are "a holy priesthood."

Now notice what happened in the Old Testament when they dedicated Solomon's Temple:

## 2 CHRONICLES 5:13,14

13 It came even to pass, as the trumpeters and singers were as one, to make one sound to be heard in praising and thanking the Lord; and when they lifted up their voice with the trumpets and cymbals and instruments of musick, and praised the Lord, saying, For he is good; for his mercy endureth for ever: that then the house was filled with a cloud, even the house of the Lord;
14 So that the priests could not stand to minister by reason of the cloud: for the glory of the Lord had filled the house of God.

Dear friends, there's something about being in unity in singing, in praying, in praising, and in worshipping that brings God on the scene! There is power in united prayer.

All the singers, players of musical instruments, priests, and everyone else present at the dedication of Solomon's Temple lifted up their voices — *all of them* — with one accord to make one sound. Evidently the singers sang the phrase, *"For he is good; for his mercy endureth for ever...."* over and over again. *Then* the House of the Lord was filled with the glory of God, and the priests could not stand to minister, because the cloud filled the house.

Is God any less good *now* than He was *then?* I remember a number of years ago when Brother Oral Roberts popularized the statement, "God is a good God." I'd often follow him in meetings in those days (and I had my best meetings in those churches where I did follow him).

But nearly every one of those pastors would say to me, "I wish Brother Roberts wouldn't say that!"

I'd reply, "Why? *Isn't* God a good God?"

"Well, yes," they said. "But it leaves *the wrong impression.*"

"What do you mean, it leaves the wrong impression?"

"Well, it just makes it *too easy* for people to get saved and healed."

I'd say, "Why, no. It doesn't make it *easier* for people to get saved and healed. Jesus did that a long time before Brother Roberts ever came on the scene, glory to God!"

Is God a good God — or is He half good and
half bad? Thank God, He's good. Glory to God,
He's GOOD! For the Lord is GOOD, and His
mercy endureth forever.

I'll tell you, when those musicians and
singers got in one accord and lifted up their
voices in praise and worship at the dedication
of Solomon's Temple, it brought the glory into
manifestation, and the glory filled that Temple.

Now let's look at something in the Acts of
the Apostles. You will recall how Peter and
John went into the Temple at 3 o'clock one
afternoon — the hour of prayer — through the
gate called Beautiful. Sitting by the gate was
a man who had been lame from birth, but he
was healed when Peter told him, *". . . In the
name of Jesus Christ of Nazareth rise up and
walk"* (Acts 3:6). Spectators marveled at the
miracle, so Peter and John used the occasion
to preach. They were soon taken before a coun-
cil of religious rulers, questioned, threatened,
and commanded not to speak or teach in the
Name of Jesus.

### ACTS 4:23,24
23 And being let go, they [Peter and John] went to
their own company [Bless God, that's the best place
to be when you get in trouble — with your own

company. I don't know about you, but I like the company I run with, glory to God.], **and reported all that the chief priests and elders had said unto them.**
**24 And when they [the believers] heard that, they lifted up their voice to God WITH ONE ACCORD, and said, Lord, thou art God, which hast made heaven, and earth, and the sea, and all that in them is.**

Notice this company of believers didn't start by bemoaning their situation or asking for anything. They didn't start with the "gimmes."

There's something about God . . . there's something about His character . . . there's something about His personality . . . there's something about His makeup which we need to learn. He manifests Himself when He is magnified and worshipped.

Notice in the Old Testament, when they lifted up their voices with one accord, saying *"For he is good; for his mercy endureth for ever,"* they weren't talking about themselves. They were talking about the Lord. God manifested His glory when the people began to magnify Him.

And notice the prayer that Peter, John, and their company prayed here in Acts 4. They began by saying, *". . . Lord, thou art God!"* They began to talk about God, to worship Him, and to lift Him up. This is what they said:

ACTS 4:24-31

24 And ... they lifted up their voice to God with one accord, and said, Lord, thou art God, which hast made heaven, and earth, and the sea, and all that in them is:
25 Who by the mouth of thy servant David hast said, Why did the heathen rage, and the people imagine vain things?
26 The kings of the earth stood up, and the rulers were gathered together against the Lord, and against his Christ.
27 For of a truth against thy holy child Jesus, whom thou hast anointed, both Herod, and Pontius Pilate, with the Gentiles, and the people of Israel, were gathered together.
28 For to do whatsoever thy hand and thy counsel determined before to be done. [First they talked about who God is and how big He is.]
29 And now, Lord, behold their threatenings: and grant unto thy servants, that with all boldness they may speak thy word.
30 By stretching forth thine hand to heal; and that signs and wonders may be done by the name of thy holy child Jesus.
31 And when they had prayed, the place was shaken where they were assembled together; and THEY WERE ALL FILLED WITH THE HOLY GHOST, and they spake the word of God with boldness.

Now, listen! Each individual was filled with

the Holy Spirit, so that *body of believers* was the *temple* of God. They were in *one* accord, and that *body* was filled with the Holy Spirit.

We all have the Holy Spirit dwelling in us — every born-again person has the Holy Spirit dwelling in him.

You can be *filled* with the Holy Spirit and speak with other tongues. On the other hand, there is something else to see from this passage of Scripture: *They* were *all*, as a *body* of believers, filled with the Holy Spirit — just like the glory of God filled the *physical house* known as Solomon's Temple.

Do you see this? Here's this *spiritual house* made up of the body of believers, and the Holy Spirit filled that "house." They were *all* filled! And what happened? The place was shaken, it says in verse thirty-one. Bless God, the place where they were assembled was *shaken!*

People get excited when a person gets full of the Holy Spirit and begins to shake or fall over. You wait, bless God, until the building starts shaking!

Sometimes in our crusades I'll see the glory come in and fill the building. Other people often see it; sometimes quite a few people. At times, it looks like a layer of clouds, like a haze, or like thick, white fog hanging right over the people's heads. Or, sometimes I've seen the glory of God manifest like a wind.

The Bible talks about the Holy Spirit manifesting Himself like a wind. He did on the Day of Pentecost:

ACTS 2:1,2
1 And when the day of Pentecost was fully come, they were all with one accord in one place.
2 And suddenly there came a sound from heaven as of A RUSHING MIGHTY WIND, and it filled all the house where they were sitting.

I was once in a service where every person in the building was instantly healed, and it occurred when the Holy Spirit manifested Himself as a wind. I'm expecting to be in more services like this in the not-too-distant future. This particular service took place some years ago in an Assemblies of God church down in East Texas. I was preaching a revival there, and the presbyter asked if I'd preach at a fellowship meeting being held in the same church. So I preached one morning service, and just as I finished my sermon, I spoke with other tongues and the pastor stood up and interpreted it. Then I spoke again with tongues and the pastor stood up again and interpreted it.

And just as his interpretation ceased, something like wind blew through that building. Everybody heard it: WHOOOSH! And everybody was instantly healed — including a woman lying by one wall on a stretcher. She jumped off that stretcher and started running down the aisle!

Later the pastor told me that doctors had operated on this woman six times, but had given her up to die. She looked the very picture of death. I remember: I saw her on that stretcher, but no one laid hands on her.

The pastor and the presbyter told me later that every sick person in the building was healed. I've only had that happen one time, but I have had other services where every lost person and every backslider got saved.

Have we forgotten about the wind? Have we forgotten about the cloud? Have we forgotten about the glory? Have we forgotten about the manifestations of the Holy Spirit? No! We refuse to forget! We believe that we shall again see the glory of God fill His temple as in days gone by, and, yea, in even greater measure!

*Prayer*

We lift up our voice with one accord unto the Father God, saying unto Him, You are God!

You are the Creator of the universe. You are
He who has made the world and all that therein
is. You are *good!* And your mercy endures
forever. You manifest yourself among men.

Yea, come manifest yourself in our midst!
We are *your* building. We are *your* house. We
are *your* temple. Come, fill your temple. Fill
your temple — the body of believers — with
your glory. Fill your temple with your glory.
Fill your house — the body of believers — with
your glory. For the body of believers is *your*
house, lively stones, the holy priesthood.